I'm Called to Preach: Now What?
Work Book

Dr. Aaron Chapman

authorHOUSE®

AuthorHouse™
1663 Liberty Drive
Bloomington, IN 47403
www.authorhouse.com
Phone: 1 (800) 839-8640

Published by AuthorHouse 05/19/2017

ISBN: 978-1-5246-9239-1 (sc)
ISBN: 978-1-5246-9238-4 (e)

Contents

Let's Get it Started

So you have the question looming in your mind likened unto other newly called preachers. You know the question… Where do I start? That is not a question of ignorance but rather a question of intelligence. You have to have a realistic view of where you are before you can determine where to begin. With this initial worksheet we will need to get you acclimated to the process of Homiletics so that we can successfully bring out the quality messages which God has placed on the inside of you.

Position: The first thing that we have to be sure of is where we are not? This in turn informs us of where we are now. Although God has called you to preach, it does not make you an authority or an expert on the subject of the gospel. Many Preachers make the mistake of believing that because they have received the call that they are now more knowledgeable and equipped than their Pastor, which often times is not the case. You yet need grooming! You may ask where am I - then? You should be in a spirit of gratefulness that He selected you for the task and see it as a privilege.

Give a short summary of your calling experience:

What events transpired to make you come into this conclusion?

What series of confirmations have taken place?

Who did you consult for wise council?

How much did you pray following the call over your life?

What is your 'why' for preaching?

Assignment: write out a one page document of your calling experience. This reflection of the experience will bring you back to what is important and why you have been called to such a task.

Personality: What are the gifts that you currently possess? Christian Palmer calls it spiritual-pneumatic personality. Preachers sometimes get so wrapped up in what they desire to obtain that they fail to take inventory of the gifts, talents and skills already present in them. Take the time and list the gifts and talents that you have at present that can be helpful to your ministry.

Example: Articulate; the advantage of being articulate is that you are clear in your vocality and communication. This helps in the delivery of the sermonic presentation at several levels.

Make a list of these gifts, talents and skills. Engage in this exercise for two reasons; first to remind yourself that you have something to offer; secondly it lets you know what you do not have so that you can seek mentorship and develop a heart and will to get better.

Possessions: Ministry is an investment. There are a couple of things that you are going to need on the journey of preaching. First, you need a study Bible. The New Interpreters study Bible is a necessity. This study Bible has commentary, and historical and literary background information. Second, you need to have some type of processing system be it computer, laptop, desktop, or tablet. If this is not in your budget you need to purchase a hard drive just for sermon prep and composition notebooks so that you can capture ideas. Do not mix your notes with other work from other research efforts or materials. This is exclusively for the preparation of the sermon.

Collect the voices

When you are trying to create a message of some kind be it a speech, a sermon, or to write a book there must be a collecting of the voices. What gives you the (ethos) credibility to speak? When you take the time to research this reveals that you honor the process and that your ideas aren't shaped in novelty. Therefore we need to take out the time to research in order to filter your ideas to assure that there is a solid foundation to stand on theologically.

How do I research for a sermon? It is very important that you have access to the right materials necessary to produce the type of product or sermon you desire. There are some necessities that can't be compromise if you want to produce a quality message. As the old saying goes, you get what you pay for. The same is true with research you receive at the same level the quality of your research and reading.

Step One: Create a list of scholars or theologians that are credible in the area of your research.

Step Two: You should take a look at books, articles and scholarly periodic journals.

Step Three: The third step is the most important you have to capture the ideas that are pertinent to what you desire to include in the document. There must be a filing system for these findings. Such as placing them in a notebook or typing the notes on a laptop or tablet. There must be an organized process for you.

Step Four: Give credit to those whom you have gleaned these ideas. Plagiarism is dishonest and dishonorable. Letting the audience hear in your document you consulted the voices will be a refreshing experience to attentive hearers.

Here is a lay out of what you should concentrate on:

Book Title
Name of the Author(s)
Subject Matter Researching
Particular Key Quotes
What other sources are found in the back of the source such as References or Bibliography.

How many hours are you willing to invest in searching out these materials? It takes time to discover quality materials.

What is the speed and or comprehension level of your reading?

Who can you discuss this information with and teach them how to personally internalize it?

Be careful of writers that have their own biases. Therefore, you must be diverse in selection of materials and the ethnicity of the authors.

Discover if there are any new books or papers that are scholarly that have been researched on the proposed topic.

Check with resources in antiquity that can give a better ancient prospective on the text.

Getting back To the Basics of Preaching

Fundamentals

Prayer:
Have you established a praying ground for yourself? The power in your preaching is based on the intensity of your prayer life.

What time will you set aside for prayer? Pray for your walk with God; pray for your ministry and pray for the enhancement of your homiletic skill and gifting.

Prioritize the Scriptures:
Thirst for reading the scriptures. This probably would for some, be a given in ministry. I believe that we have to get back to reading the book.

Construct a reading plan that you will devote yourself to for your spiritual and sermonic growth.

My suggestion for reading the bible is to read four chapters daily.

Preaching Practitioners:

Listen to Preaching everyday. At least take the time to listen to one sermon a day.

Foundations

Take time out and research the background of the Early Church Fathers of Homiletics: John Chrysostom, Augustine, Martin Luther, Charles Spurgeon and Alexander Maclaren.

Study Philosophers and the arrangements of arguments in order that you may be able to see the sequence of how arguments are built.

Features

To every sermonic style there are features. We need to explore the features to Expository Preaching and Exposition and many others.

Define in your own words these formats of preaching

1. Preaching
2. Narrative Preaching
3. Topical Preaching
4. Textual Preaching
5. Theological Integrity and Accuracy

6. Expository
7. Exposition

Passion

What is inside of you that drives you to preach? What is your 'why' in preaching?

From a scale of 1 to 10 where is your commitment for preaching currently. Does the time you put in reflect the answer that was given?

If you could define preaching in one word what would it be?

Preparation

Draft a reading schedule for preaching books alone.

What goals do you have for particular areas of your preaching this year?

What are you willing to budget each year so that you have funds to buy resources?

How much time would you say you need to work to perfect your craft?

Do you love the platform of preaching more than the process?

What steps are you taking to make your preparation time a priority?

Psychological

Confidence is a major key to preaching. What are some positive things that you recognize in your preaching?

What are current distractions that are apprehending your time for growth? Examples: television, face book, telephone calls, proving others wrong, or any other distractions?

Developing mental toughness has to be a priority. You can be gifted but yet afraid or mentally unstable which prevents your excelling at the level of your ability because you haven't quite matured mentally.

Chapter 1

Do Not Despise the Process

Inspiration is Easy. Implementation Is the Hard Part

Bob Taylor

What are some of the greatest temptation to the preacher?

Have you leaned on your talent more then your work ethic? How can we change this mindset?

Fill in the blanks:

The preacher must first fall in love with _____

The preacher should secondly fall in love with _____

Lastly, the preacher should fall in love with _____

What is Studying according to Fred Craddock?

Study is getting a second and third _____

_____

Writers Block vs. Confidence Block

Are you a victim of confidence block? Have you ever thought this is a stupid idea or possibly no one wants to hear what I have to say because I don't have all of those words and I'm not gifted with vocal variety like others. This causes confidence block that appears to be writers block. How do you solve it?

Repetition- the more you write sermons the better you will improve. It is just that simple.

Renovation of your thoughts- you have to remove yourself from negative or pessimistic thoughts.

Refueling- Sometimes we run out of ideas because we have not filled the tank up with our exposure to the right material or messages which aid in our gleaning inspiration.

Killers of Confidence

- I can't
- I don't have
- That's just the way it is
- No one will help me
- I'm wasting my time
- Why can't I do it like them?
- What's the use?

Builders of Confidence

- I know the Lord called me
- I surely can
- I love a challenge
- Let's get it
- Let's go

- God you are in Control
- Help Holy Spirit
- I am made to do this
- I am unstoppable
- The Spirit of the Lord is upon me.

What are the excuses that you have made? List them here:

Now that we have this list of what is stopping us we can stop using these crutches and move on in ministry.

Who is your inspiration? You should have someone who when looking at their situation you're encouraged and can draw inspiration from them when you're facing challenges. This will encourage you to not quit the process.

How is your Temple doing? Our bodies are the temple of God! *1 Cor. 6:19*

What exercise regiment have you implemented? Is it the right one for the type of ministry you're performing?

Here are some suggestions

Monday: leg exercises

Tuesday: arm exercises

Wednesday: back exercises

Thursday: abdominal exercises

Friday: chest exercises

Run every other day long distance to keep the heart rate going

Food for Thought

The food that we ingest is very important aid us with where we desire our energy level to be.

We should eat at minimum three meals a day

*******Lessen your sugar intake*******

What amount of time are you resting to reenergize your body for the journey? If you do not receive the proper amount of rest the body will shut down on you.

Chapter 2

Determining your Paradigm of Preaching

*Ministry can be fruitful only if it grows out of a
direct and intimate encounter with our Lord
Mother Teresa*

What is your working definition for preaching?

Create a non-negotiable statement of your values as a preacher. This statement is something you will live by and will become a reminder to you to remain on track.

We must remember that preaching is a God Ordained transaction.

Preaching has its own language so we must acquaint ourselves with that language. Define these words or terms:

- Homiletics

- Exegesis

- Eisegesis

- Pericope

- Inductive Preaching

- Deductive Preaching

Listed below are books that you ought to have within reaching distance while studying:

- Study Bible
- Parallel Bible
- Bible Dictionary
- Manners and Customs
- English Dictionary(or Primary Language)
- Thesaurus
- Illustrative Book

Now list the importance of each book to the sermonic preparation process.

Sermonic Bridge

Every sermon in which we preach must be done in a way that it enables individuals to conquer the gulf that is between them and God.

The sermonic bridge is a picture of what transpires in services and gatherings across the country. With every new sermon there is a new bridge that is created. Therefore it becomes our job to place in the hearts of men and women the original intent of what is in the heart of God. Here is an example in diagram **1.1 of the bridge**

Sermonic Bridge

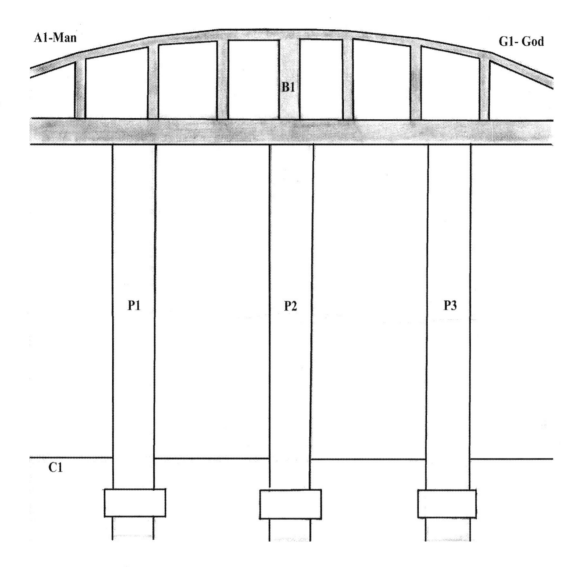

As it is noted in diagram one - A 1 represents the position of man. G1 represents the presence of God. B1 is the Bridge which is necessary for us to cross to have salvation or understanding of his word.

P1, P2, P3 are representations of the points which are the beams that support the bridge

C1 is the foundation that allows the bridge to remain unmoved which is the Holy Spirit.

Study the text not only as a good scholar but also as an honest struggler.

Chapter 3

Developing Original Thought in Sermon Preparation

*"Study the text not only as a good scholar
but also as an honest struggler"*

Larry Crabb

Create a schedule of study for consistency

Sunday
Monday
Tuesday
Wednesday
Thursday
Friday
Saturday

Methodology defined- a system of methods used in a particular area of study or activity and is essential in producing consistent messages.

What is your current method of scripture interpretation? In two paragraphs, write out the process which you've previously gone through in the past.

Argument of Preaching- As preachers we must defend the faith and the unsearchable truths of God. Apologetics in the New Testament comprises a study of the art of persuasion employed by the early Christian Church. The context among Jewish and Hellenistic thought and laid a foundation for the 2nd Century apologists.

The importance of Rhetoric- The arguments that are being constructed for preaching finds its baring in Philosophical arguments. You can find this style in the Pauline writings and others writings that have structure to prove or disprove a particular point. Therefore it is beneficial for us to know about rhetoric.

- **Exordium**- (Introduction) striving for attention

- **Narratio** - describe the context or the background

- **Propositio** - This is the proposition or the big idea or claim

- **Probatio** - this is the main body to the argument

- **Refutatio** - disproving the oppositions arguments

- **Peroratio** - the conclusion and summary; appealing to the audiences emotions.

Exordium- This is the introduction of the argument or sermon

    A. Diverse- You should not use the same method to present the introduction. For example, do not always open with my brothers and sisters, do not always open with saying church, don't always open with beloved. Make the introduction diverse so that it remains fresh and interesting to the audience.

    B. Divine- Your introduction should clarify how we can see the Theos or God in this introduction.

    C. Domestic- You should meet the people where they are in the sermon. If the people can't detect their involvement they will become discouraged listeners.

Narratio - This is where we give the background information that is necessary to place us in the scene of the scripture. We are foreigners to the text when we first read it so we need to give the essential things in the sermon so we can cross over from antiquity to the contemporary. This is what is articulated in Grasping God's Word as the Principlizing Bridge.

Propositio - This is the Big idea, the Main idea, the Sermonic claim in the words of Dr. Marvin McMickle. This part of the sermon is the direction of the sermon that we have consented to go in. Capture what is burning and bothering you on the inside.

Refutatio - This word is to disprove the arguments that are already in place. What are the claims that the congregation may have in their minds that you have to disprove? It could possibly be the claim that they shouldn't do it God's way.

Probatio - The supporting arguments to the proposition. The probatio is the beams that I spoke about earlier for the sermonic bridge each beam is a supporting argument to the main point.

Peroratio - In this section there is an appeal. When there are marching orders put in place we have to make the appeal to bring them to a place of decision so as to discover if they will take the necessary steps.

Now we will turn to the Sermonic Structure in order that we can develop it fully through practice.

Define a Thesis:

Example of a Thesis: Christ can get up your Dead Stuff

Give Three Thesis Statements and Select Accurate scripture

1.
2.
3.

Define Antithesis

Example of an Antithesis: Christ has given you unlimited favor in the abundance of life

Give Three Antithesis Statements and Select the accurate scripture

1.
2.
3.

Take one of the texts from above and engage in the following:

Investigation- In this step we want to question the text and write down the details

Explanation- Here you should give your initial observations but being open for them to be redefined

Illustration- Give an example through a story or circumstance that can make it practical to the hearing by shedding light on it from some of the points you are driving home.

Application- What is it from the Biblical Writ that rings true from this passage in the contemporary setting? How does it apply to us in the domestic setting?

Manifestation- This component deals with the transferring of the biblical knowledge into the area of our lives, where we can do something with it that's tangible; so that others can feel it in their lives.

Chapter 4

Day One acquainting yourself with the Text

**I seen words in sentences, I have seen words misspelled,
I have seen words misinterpreted but on Calvary this was
the first time I ever saw a word bleed. When you preach
do we see the Word bleeding for our salvation?**

- Rev. Joseph Chapman

Do you have a designated area for studying the scriptures? There must be a ground that is consecrated for the work of the Lord.

The question that you are probably asking yourself is "where do I start?" Here is a running list of things that you will need:

- Desk or table
- Book shelves
- Scholarly sources
- Prayer area
- Note books
- Computer or Laptop
- Typing paper

Printed Symbols that remind you of the mission

De-clutter- a cluttered work area is a reflection of a cluttered mind.

2: Timothy 2:5 rightly dividing the word of truth. Orthotemeiv is a compound word temeiv which means to cut and ortho means straight. We are to give it to the people straight.

Have you ever struggled with compromising the text because you have not spent sufficient time?

What were the challenges that brought you to the place where you were not able to give substantial time to the task?

There needs to be a designated day as the starting point for sermon development. Which day will you start your preparation.

What is your method of selecting the passages or pericopes that you would like to preach?

How can you improve on the method of selecting scriptures?

What commitment are you willing to make to ensure that you don't waste valuable time in sermonic study?

Chapter 5

Day Two Building The Bridge

A talk (sermon) is a voyage. It must be charted.
The speaker (Preacher) who starts nowhere usually gets there.

-Dale Carnegie

The sermon needs to have a singularity in focus

Many ideas may come to you during the time of preparation but we need to sacrifice the innumerable minor points of the sermon so that we can communicate the major point.

Follow the worksheet below to keep you organized.

Characters in the Passage:

_____

_____

_____

_____

_____

What are some of the Doctrinal Themes that peak your interest:

_____

_____

_____

_____

_____

Why have you been drawn to this scripture in the first place and is it still in your spirit?

When there appears to be too much information for one sermon this could be a great indicator that you may need to do a series of sermons.

One of the methodologies that have been impactful for exegesis is questioning the text. Here are the six questions you should ask the text:

Who

What

When

Where

Why

How

See Figure 3

Who?	What?	When?	Where?	How?	Why?
God	Loved	Believeth	World	Love	Not perish
World	Gave		In Him	Gave	Love
His	Only			Believeth	Everlasting-life
Son	Believeth			In him	
Whosoever	Perish				
Him	Everlasting-Life				

Sermonic Puzzle Pieces

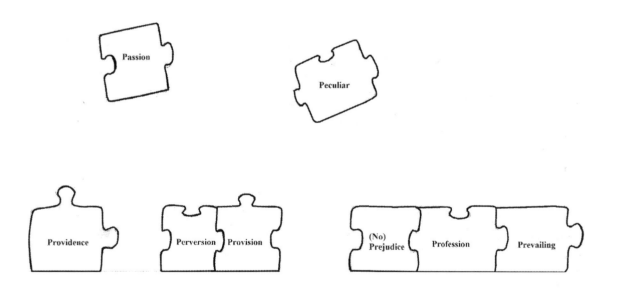

View the layout of the sermon and research as if finding pieces to the puzzle. The proposition is the picture on the box that shows us exactly how it should look. Below you will find an example of this based on John 3:16

Figure 4 (Have this figure created for the sermon on John 3:16) **Puzzle Pieces**

The Proposition as stated earlier is a very important key to what you are doing in the sermon. Here we will take the opportunity to give exercises on the proposition.

Step 1 When crafting a proposition the language needs to have similarities to the text language that is already present. What I mean by this is interchange the wording in the text in order to make the communication clear and yet concise.

Step 2 The length of the proposition needs to be only 1 to 2 sentences at most. The proposition should be meticulous in its crafting so feel it not strange to write this statement over 5 to 10 times or more. You need to take your time so that you tighten the statement where there are no unnecessary words that are lingering out there that don't have to be communicated because you already have the point without them.

Step 3 Is the language that you are using scholarly and congregant appropriate because we have to make sure that it is understandable. The whole goal of the proposition is to simplify the dynamics of the sermon in one phrase. Can they get the whole sermon in one phrase?

Step 4 The proposition must be relevant to the audience to whom you will be preaching this sermon. When you are preparing "you have to do what Pastor Sandy Ray of the Cornerstone Baptist Church use to say and that is that you need to go grocery shopping" so that you may have something that meets the theological diet necessary but not condensing to people's fickle whims of secularity.

Step 5 You have to choose what mountain you are going to live and die on. What this sermon's possible one shot will rise and fall on. You must have commitment to the proposition and see it through to the end.

Step 6 Don't complicate the drafting of the proposition. Get the ideas on paper and then go from there but don't become so generic that there is a lack of innovation and autonomy. In other words just write it and write it well.

Thesis

You need to have a thesis that is birthed from the proposition. The proposition and the Thesis should have a similar sound and a similar aim; they should not be all over the place. They must be connected so that they may be choreographed very smoothly through the sermon.

Joann Deitz remarked of the thesis that it should have focus and organization around a central idea. The thesis is the main point. It ask the question of the 'so what' and 'why' is this idea and sermon necessary?

Anti-thesis

Antithesis is the opposite of the Thesis.

When we are drafting an Antithesis, sometimes there might not be a word that is the total opposite but we can draft a concept that has the tone of the opposite.

When drafting Antithesis it must be something that we can raise as a problem in the passage.

The Antithesis is just as important as the Thesis. We need to spend just as much time on the Antithesis as we do the Thesis.

Preferable the Antithesis should be what begins your introduction because people in the congregation appear to be more interested in the problem initially. At which time you can then get them to see that there are solutions for the problems.

Tension in the Text

Let me say from the outset that we have to be careful with this phrase 'Tension in the Text.' Some of us get addicted to problems and we create one that is not even present in order that we can appear to be deep. I heard on occasion that a young preacher was speaking of Mark 4 and the text says that Jesus was asleep on the boat and the tension was supposedly that how can Jesus sleep when he never slumbers nor sleep according to the Old Testament of Psalms 121. We have to beware of these theological tragedies.

Raise problems throughout a pericope to keep people thinking with you while unveiling an oasis of revelation that was birthed through the sermonic preparation process.

Chapter 6

Day Three the Meat of the Message Drafting Points

What makes a sermonic Master piece is not what you put in the sermon it is what you strategically leave out of the sermon.

- Rev. Tellis Chapman

What great preaching minds have you made yourself available to?

When you are hearing the great orators and expositors you can't become so enthralled with their eloquence that you miss their executing exegetically.

Some of the things that you should pay attention to are as follows:

The technique
The names that they are quoting (you should read them as well)
What are they doing repetitiously?
What is the pace of the presentation?
What is there eye contact like?
How do they connect with different audiences?
Just hearing a preacher preaching should not satisfy the curiosity that you possess.

Karl Barth says that it is already a tough task to think, but it is even tougher to think about how we think, but the toughest task is to teach how others think about how you should think and that is homiletics.

When you listen to preaching don't just think about what it has done to you but how did this happen to you.

Match the verbs with the pronouns

Exercise 1

Exodus 1:8 concerning the arising of a new Pharaoh

Pharaoh:

Arose- Elevation
Did not know Joseph- Egotism
He said to his people Look-Evaluation
Let us deal shrewdly- Expectation

This is just an example of how you can construct points from the movements of a specific character in the text or pericope.

Select a text that has a minimum of three Characters and match up the verbs with the nouns

What homiletic ingredients comprise a strong point?

1st - the point needs to be derive from proper exegesis; does this idea come from the text?

2nd - preach the points in chronological order or the progression of the natural movements of the text.

3rd - The points should build on each other. There should be a natural progression to the message. It should be moving toward a destination or climax.

4th - You should grab your grocery cart and go shopping. You must know the audience so that you can communicate in their language. You should know the social ills or the economical deprivation etc.

5th - Always remember that Context is King and Queen. You want to make sure the point that you are trying to convey makes sense contextually.

6th - Content - Be careful of the content that you are using All the information that is in a text book is not necessarily scholarly.

7th – Connections - Use supporting scripture as an addition to but not as the exclusive main attraction; if this is the case you should have preached the text you keep referring to oppose to the public read text that was selected.

8th - Compartmentalized; the person that hears the message that has been given should be able to take the package with them and know how to use it when they get home. This is the part of theology that we must always include in our sermonic delivery so that we can make something happen with what we've just heard. If not, it might possibly mean that the way the sermon was packaged might not have been in the proper container so as to bare the contents for future use which unfortunately means that it is worthless to the hearer.

Chapter 7

Day Four Refine thoughts through Commentary and Etymology Study

Adversity is the first path to truth.

Poet Lord Byron

As a beginner or an advanced exegete, you need to have tools at your disposal. My Father, Rev. Joseph Chapman, used to tell me to treat books like a tool box. You might not need the tool immediately but when the right situations arise, you will have it readily available, opposed to needing it and having to go and find it.

What are the most important tools that you will need in your preaching tool box?

Commentaries - When you look for Commentaries look for scholarly commentaries. The writers normally are teaching at particular seminaries or universities this is very important. These writers have been critiqued by their peers and across the world which means they have been tried.

The second piece to purchasing a good commentary is making sure that it is not too dated because there are archaeological digs that have took place following those publications and you want to aim for biblical accuracy.

Lastly, make sure that you read the entire commentary on your passage and not stop because you have found something that leans toward your line of theological thinking. This is very important because sometimes the commentary writer can express that this was a scholars view but highly unlikely. You want to be thorough in the reading and not make careless mistakes by trying to rush the process.

What should you write down from the commentary?

- Quotes relevant to the point you're trying to make.

- Dates of when the book was written or when the event took place.

- The interpretation of the names of those places mentioned

- The dismissal of flawed traditions that have been straighten out in the commentary

You want to write down what goes on within the direction of your sermon and be open to the challenging of your myopic view on a pericope.

You need to make up within your mind that it is worth it to spend a large sum of money on books for preparatory purposes because trust me, the money spent will yield great dividends in all areas of ministry.

Refer to Chapter 7 in the book about the different levels of commentaries and which ones are appropriate for where you are currently within the ministry.

Chapter 8

Day Five Introduction and
Putting the Pieces together.

Procrastination is opportunity's natural assassin

Victor Kiam

Introductions

I believe that one of the most underestimated parts of a sermon is the introduction. There are those that squander the entire sermon on a careless introduction that took little to no thought.

What should be included in an effective introduction?

There should be an attention getter. This means something that is thought provoking but not something that is trying to create shock effect. I have seen preachers that seem to have an infatuation with the shock effect. They will begin to stretch and bend the truth just to create it every time which is not healthy for the spirituality of the congregation.

Diversity is key don't use the same phrases in order to open up every single time this is what allows for your introduction to be predictable and this becomes a turn off.

Current events that match the direction of a sermon are great!

Illustrations that are partially given at the beginning, and then use the remainder of the illustration at the end; this helps bring the sermon full circle and is a great method.

What are ineffective ways of introducing a sermon?

Note: Definitions from the English dictionary are not always equal to biblical meanings!

Starting a sermon by saying… In our text today - this doesn't take any creativity; you need to dig deeper!

Using a revivalist story that everyone knows and changing the story or getting the story wrong;

Using words just to sound deep but lose the connection with the congregation;

Being Dogmatic from the outset;

We all have room for improvement but we need to pay close attention to the concepts and methods we can use to engage the congregation that can move them from the introduction to the body of the sermon.

If you do what is easy your life will be hard. If you do what is hard your life will be easy.

Les Brown

Remember: Go and Be Great DR.A.L. CHAPMAN

Notes

Notes

Notes

Notes

Notes

Notes

Notes

Notes

Notes

Notes

Notes

Notes

Notes

Notes

Notes

Printed in the United States
By Bookmasters